FAVORITE POEMS
of the SEA

A COASTAL COLLECTION

Published by Bushel & Peck Books, a family-run publishing house in Fresno, California,
that believes in uplifting children with the highest standards of art, music, literature, and
ideas. Find beautiful books for gifted young minds at www.bushelandpeckbooks.com.

Type set in Temeraire and Baskerville.
Shell engravings by Marzufello/Shutterstock.com

Designed by David Miles.

Bushel & Peck Books is dedicated to fighting illiteracy all over the world. For every
book we sell, we donate one to a child in need—book for book. To nominate a school or
organization to receive free books, please visit www.bushelandpeckbooks.com.

ISBN: 9781638191032

First Edition

Printed in the United States

10 9 8 7 6 5 4 3 2 1

FAVORITE
POEMS
of the SEA

A COASTAL COLLECTION

BUSHEL
& PECK
BOOKS

CONTENTS

FULL FATHOM FIVE

William Shakespeare

Full fathom five thy father lies;
Of his bones are coral made;
Those are pearls that were his eyes:
Nothing of him that doth fade,
But doth suffer a sea-change
Into something rich and strange.
Sea-nymphs hourly ring his knell:

Ding-dong.

Hark! now I hear them,—Ding-dong, bell.

BREAK, BREAK, BREAK

Alfred, Lord Tennyson

Break, break, break,
On thy cold gray stones, O Sea!
And I would that my tongue could utter
The thoughts that arise in me.

O well for the fisherman's boy,
That he shouts with his sister at play!
O well for the sailor lad,
That he sings in his boat on the bay!

And the stately ships go on
To their haven under the hill;
But O for the touch of a vanish'd hand,
And the sound of a voice that is still!

Break, break, break,
At the foot of thy crags, O Sea!
But the tender grace of a day that is dead
Will never come back to me.

OREAD

Hilda Doolittle

Whirl up, sea—
Whirl your pointed pines,
Splash your great pines
On our rocks,
Hurl your green over us,
Cover us with your pools of fir.

THE OCEAN OF SONG

Ella Wheeler Wilcox

In a land beyond sight or conceiving,
   In a land where no blight is, no wrong,
No darkness, no graves, and no grieving,
   There lies the great ocean of song.
And its waves, oh, its waves unbeholden
   By any save gods, and their kind,
Are not blue, are not green, but are golden,
   Like moonlight and sunlight combined.

It was whispered to me that their waters
   Were made from the gathered-up tears
That were wept by the sons and the daughters
   Of long-vanished eras and spheres.
Like white sands of heaven the spray is
   That falls all the happy day long,
And whoever it touches straightway is
   Made glad with the spirit of song.

Up, up to the clouds where their hoary
   Crowned heads melt away in the skies,
The beautiful mountains of glory
   Each side of the song-ocean rise.
Here day is one splendour of sky-light—
   Of God's light with beauty replete.
Here night is not night, but is twilight,
   Pervading, enfolding, and sweet.

Bright birds from all climes and all regions,
   That sing the whole glad summer long,
Are dumb, till they flock here in legions
   And lave in the ocean of song.
It is here that the four winds of heaven,
   The winds that do sing and rejoice,
It is here they first came and were given
   The secret of sound and a voice.

Far down along beautiful beeches,
   By night and by glorious day,
The throng of the gifted ones reaches,
   Their foreheads made white with the spray,
And a few of the sons and the daughters
   Of this kingdom, cloud-hidden from sight,

Go down in the wonderful waters,
   And bathe in those billows of light.

And their souls evermore are like fountains,
   And liquid and lucent and strong,
High over the tops of the mountains
   Gush up the sweet billows of song.
No drouth-time of waters can dry them,
   Whoever has bathed in that sea,
All dangers, all deaths, they defy them,
   And are gladder than gods are, with glee.

SEA FEVER

John Masefield

I must down to the seas again, to the lonely sea and the sky,
And all I ask is a tall ship and a star to steer her by,
And the wheel's kick and the wind's song and the white sail's
  shaking,
And a grey mist on the sea's face and a grey dawn breaking.
I must down to the seas again, for the call of the running tide
Is a wild call and a clear call that may not be denied;
And all I ask is a windy day with the white clouds flying,
And the flung spray and the blown spume, and the sea-gulls
  crying.
I must down to the seas again to the vagrant gypsy life,
To the gull's way and the whale's way where the wind's like a
  whetted knife;
And all I ask is a merry yarn from a laughing fellow-rover,
And quiet sleep and a sweet dream when the long trick's over.

STORM

Heinrich Heine

The tempest is raging.
It lashes the waves,
And the waves foaming and rearing in wrath
Tower on high, and the white mountains of water
Surge as though they were alive,
While the little ship over-climbs them
With laborious haste,
And suddenly plunges down
Into the black, wide-yawning abyss of the tide.
O sea.
Thou mother of beauty, of the foam-engendered one,
Grandmother of love, spare me!
Already scenting death, flutters around me
The white, ghostly sea-mew,
And whets his beak on the mast.
And hungers with glutton-greed for the heart

Which resounds with the glory of thy daughter,

And which the little rogue, thy grandson,

Hath chosen for his play-ground.

In vain are my prayers and entreaties,

My cry dies away in the rushing storm,

In the battle-tumult of the winds.

They roar and whistle and crackle and howl

Like a bedlam of tones.

And amidst them, distinctly I hear

Alluring notes of harps,

Heart-melting, heart-rending,

And I recognize the voice.

Far away on the rocky Scotch coast,

Where the little gray castle juts out

Over the breaking waves,—

There at the lofty-arched window

Stands a beautiful suffering woman,

Transparently delicate, and pale as marble.

And she plays on the harp, and she sings,

And the wind stirs her flowing locks,

And wafts her melancholy song

Over the wide, stormy sea.

INVOCATION FROM
A HIGH CLIFF

Cale Young Rice

Sweep unrest
Out of my blood,
Winds of the sea! Sweep the fog
Out of my brain
For I am one
Who has told Life he will be free.
Who will not doubt of work that's done,
Who will not fear the work to do,
Who will hold peaks Promethean
Better than all Jove's honey-dew.
Who when the Vulture tears his breast
Will smile into the Terror's Eyes.
Who for the World has this Bequest—
Hope, that eternally is wise.

NIGHT

Cora C. Bass

The mellow moonbeams glint along the waves,

Beyond the inky blur yon frowning height

Full oft impresses on the tranquil deep.

What eagle glances pierce the veil of gloom!

Each galaxy of light proclaims a town,

Instinct with life, as childhood is with joy.

Afar, like some dim phantom of the hour,

A liner speeds majestic on her way;

While beaconward a schooner lies at ease,

A graceful shadow on a silvered sea.

TEMPEST

Heinrich Heine

Gloomy lowers the tempest over the sea,

And through the black wall of cloud

Is unsheathed the jagged lightning,

Swift outflashing, and swift-vanishing,

Like a jest from the brain of Chronos.

Over the barren, billowy water,

Far away rolls the thunder,

And up leap the white water-steeds,

Which Boreas himself begot

Out of the graceful mare of Erichthon,

And the sea-birds flutter around,

Like the shadowy dead on the Styx,

Whom Charon repels from his nocturnal boat.

Poor, merry, little vessel,

Dancing yonder the most wretched of dances!

Eolus sends it his liveliest comrades,

Who wildly play to the jolliest measures;
One pipes his horn, another blows,
A third scrapes his growling bass-viol.
And the uncertain sailor stands at the rudder,
And constantly gazes at the compass,
The trembling soul of the ship;
And he raises his hands in supplication to Heaven—
"Oh, save me, Castor, gigantic hero!
And thou conquering wrestler, Pollux."

THE CITY IN THE SEA

Edgar Allen Poe

Lo! Death has reared himself a throne
In a strange city lying alone
Far down within the dim West,
Where the good and the bad and the worst and the best
Have gone to their eternal rest.
There shrines and palaces and towers
(Time-eaten towers that tremble not)
Resemble nothing that is ours.
Around, by lifting winds forgot,
Resignedly beneath the sky
The melancholy waters lie.

No rays from the holy heaven come down
On the long night-time of that town;
But light from out the lurid sea
Streams up the turrets silently,
Gleams up the pinnacles far and free:

Up domes, up spires, up kingly halls,
Up fanes, up Babylon-like walls,

Up shadowy long-forgotten bowers
Of sculptured ivy and stone flowers,
Up many and many a marvellous shrine
Whose wreathed friezes intertwine
The viol, the violet, and the vine.
Resignedly beneath the sky
The melancholy waters lie.
So blend the turrets and shadows there
That all seem pendulous in air,
While from a proud tower in the town
Death looks gigantically down.

There open fanes and gaping graves
Yawn level with the luminous waves;
But not the riches there that lie
In each idol's diamond eye,—
Not the gaily-jewelled dead,
Tempt the waters from their bed;
For no ripples curl, alas,
Along that wilderness of glass;

No swellings tell that winds may be
Upon some far-off happier sea;
No heavings hint that winds have been
On seas less hideously serene!

But lo, a stir is in the air!
The wave—there is a movement there!
As if the towers had thrust aside,
In slightly sinking, the dull tide;
As if their tops had feebly given
A void within the filmy Heaven!
The waves have now a redder glow,
The hours are breathing faint and low;
And when, amid no earthly moans,
Down, down that town shall settle hence,
Hell, rising from a thousand thrones,
Shall do it reverence.

SEA-CHANGE

John Masefield

'Goneys an' gullies an' all o' the birds o' the sea,
They ain't no birds, not really,' said Billy the Dane.
Not mollies, nor gullies, nor goneys at all,' said he,
'But simply the sperrits of mariners livin' again.

'Them birds goin' fishin' is nothin' but souls o' the drowned,
Souls o' the drowned an' the kicked as are never no more;
An' that there haughty old albatross cruisin' around,
Belike he's Admiral Nelson or Admiral Noah.

An' merry's the life they are living. They settle and dip,
They fishes, they never stands watches, they waggle their wings;
When a ship comes by, they fly to look at the ship
To see how the nowaday mariners manages things.

'When freezing aloft in a snorter, I tell you I wish—
(Though maybe it ain't like a Christian)—I wish I could be
A haughty old copper-bound albatross dipping for fish
And coming the proud over all o' the birds o' the sea.'

DOVER BEACH

Matthew Arnold

The sea is calm to-night.
The tide is full, the moon lies fair
Upon the straits; on the French coast, the light
Gleams and is gone; the cliffs of England stand,
Glimmering and vast, out in the tranquil bay.
Come to the window, sweet is the night-air!
Only, from the long line of spray
Where the sea meets the moon-blanched sand,
Listen! you hear the grating roar
Of pebbles which the waves draw back, and fling,
At their return, up the high strand,
Begin and cease, and then again begin,
With tremulous cadence slow, and bring
The eternal note of sadness in.

Sophocles long ago
Heard it on the Ægean, and it brought
Into his mind the turbid ebb and flow

Of human misery: we
Find also in the sound a thought,
Hearing it by this distant northern sea.

The sea of faith
Was once, too, at the full, and round earth's shore
Lay like the folds of a bright girdle furled.
But now I only hear
Its melancholy, long, withdrawing roar,
Retreating, to the breath
Of the night-wind, down the vast edges drear
And naked shingles of the world.

Ah, love, let us be true
To one another! for the world, which seems
To lie before us like a land of dreams,
So various, so beautiful, so new,
Hath really neither joy, nor love, nor light,
Nor certitude, nor peace, nor help for pain;
And we are here as on a darkling plain
Swept with confused alarms of struggle and flight,
Where ignorant armies clash by night.

BY THE SEA

Emily Dickinson

I started early, took my dog,
And visited the sea;
The mermaids in the basement
Came out to look at me,

And frigates in the upper floor
Extended hempen hands,
Presuming me to be a mouse
Aground, upon the sands.

But no man moved me till the tide
Went past my simple shoe,
And past my apron and my belt,
And past my bodice too,

And made as he would eat me up
As wholly as a dew

Upon a dandelion's sleeve —
And then I started too.

And he — he followed close behind;
I felt his silver heel
Upon my ankle, — then my shoes
Would overflow with pearl.

Until we met the solid town,
No man he seemed to know;
And bowing with a mighty look
At me, the sea withdrew.

THE OCEAN

Jamie Harris Coleman

O waves of the ocean since the world was created,
    You have been beating against the land;
You come and go, to and fro,
    And cleanse the grains of sand.

O ocean blue, your waves roll high,
    What a wonderful sight to behold;
The billows foam o'er the depths unknown,
    And the lives lost on you are untold.

The joy of the sailor thou art, O waves,
    Your roaring is heard far away;
You dash so high you seem to touch the sky,
    Resting not night or day.

Sailing, sailing, away goes the ship,
    Plunging thru the waves she goes;
Trying her best to stand the test,
    Whether she'll reach the harbor, who knows.

A WANDERER'S SONG

John Masefield

A wind's in the heart of me, a fire's in my heels,
I am tired of brick and stone and rumbling wagon-wheels;
I hunger for the sea's edge, the limits of the land,
Where the wild old Atlantic is shouting on the sand.

Oh I'll be going, leaving the noises of the street,
To where a lifting foresail-foot is yanking at the sheet;
To a windy, tossing anchorage where yawls and ketches ride,
Oh I'll be going, going, until I meet the tide.

And first I'll hear the sea-wind, the mewing of the gulls,
The clucking, sucking of the sea about the rusty hulls,
The songs at the capstan in the hooker warping out,
And then the heart of me'll know I'm there or thereabout.

Oh I am tired of brick and stone, the heart of me is sick,
For windy green, unquiet sea, the realm of Moby Dick;
And I'll be going, going, from the roaring of the wheels,
For a wind's in the heart of me, a fire's in my heels.

BASKING

Cale Young Rice

———

Give me a spot in the sun,
    With a lizard basking by me,
In Sicily, over the sea,
    Where Winter is sweet as Spring,
Where Etna lifts his plume
    Of curling smoke to try me,
But all in vain for I will not climb
    His height so ravishing.

Give me a spot in the sun,
    So high on a cliff that, under,
Far down, the flecking sails
    Like white moths flit the blue;
That over me on a crag
    There hangs, O aëry wonder,
A white town drowsing in its nest
    That cypress-tops peep thro.

Give me a spot in the sun,
    With contadini singing,
And a goat-boy at his pipes
    And donkey bells heard round
Upon steep mountain paths
    Where a peasant cart comes swinging
Mid joyous hot invectives—that
    So blameless here abound.

Give me a spot in the sun,
    In a land whose speech is flowers,
Whose breath is Hybla-sweet,
    Whose soul is still a faun's,
Whose limbs the sea enlaps,
    Thro long delicious hours,
With liquid tenderness and light
    Sweet as Elysian dawns.

Give me a spot in the sun
    With a view past vale and villa,
Past grottoed isle and sea
    To Italy and the Cape
Around whose turning lies
    Old heathen-hearted Scylla,
Whom may an ancient sailor prayed

The gods he might escape.

Give me a spot in the sun:
    With sly old Pan as lazy
As I, ever to tempt me
    To disbelief and doubt
Of all gods else, from Jove
    To Bacchus born wine-crazy.
Give me, I say, a spot in the sun,
    And Realms I'll do without!

THE OUTLET

Emily Dickinson

My river runs to thee:
Blue sea, wilt welcome me?

My river waits reply.
Oh sea, look graciously!

I'll fetch thee brooks
From spotted nooks, —

Say, sea,
Take me!

O CAPTAIN! MY CAPTAIN!

Walt Whitman

O Captain! my Captain! our fearful trip is done,
   The ship has weather'd every rack, the prize we sought is won;
   The port is near, the bells I hear, the people all exulting,
   While follow eyes the steady keel, the vessel grim and daring:
      But O heart! heart! heart!
       O the bleeding drops of red,
         Where on the deck my Captain lies,
            Fallen cold and dead!

O Captain! my Captain! rise up and hear the bells;
Rise up—for you the flag is flung—for you the bugle trills;
For you bouquets and ribbon'd wreaths—for you the shores
 a-crowding;
For you they call, the swaying mass, their eager faces turning;
      Here, Captain! dear father!
       This arm beneath your head;
         It is some dream that on the deck
            You've fallen cold and dead.

My Captain does not answer, his lips are pale and still;

My father does not feel my arm, he has no pulse nor will:

The ship is anchor'd safe and sound, its voyage closed and
    done;

From fearful trip the victor ship comes in with object won:

    Exult, O shores, and ring, O bells!

     But I, with mournful tread,

      Walk the deck my Captain lies,

       Fallen cold and dead.

JOHN MARR AND OTHER SAILORS

Herman Melville

Since as in night's deck-watch ye show,
Why, lads, so silent here to me,
Your watchmate of times long ago?
Once, for all the darkling sea,
You your voices raised how clearly,
Striking in when tempest sung;
Hoisting up the storm-sail cheerly,
Life is storm—let storm! you rung.
Taking things as fated merely,
Childlike though the world ye spanned;
Nor holding unto life too dearly,
Ye who held your lives in hand—
Skimmers, who on oceans four
Petrels were, and larks ashore.

O, not from memory lightly flung,
Forgot, like strains no more availing,

The heart to music haughtier strung;
Nay, frequent near me, never staleing,
Whose good feeling kept ye young.
Like tides that enter creek or stream,
Ye come, ye visit me, or seem
Swimming out from seas of faces,
Alien myriads memory traces,
To enfold me in a dream!

I yearn as ye. But rafts that strain,
Parted, shall they lock again?
Twined we were, entwined, then riven,
Ever to new embracements driven,
Shifting gulf-weed of the main!
And how if one here shift no more,
Lodged by the flinging surge ashore?
Nor less, as now, in eve's decline,
Your shadowy fellowship is mine.
Ye float around me, form and feature:—
Tattooings, ear-rings, love-locks curled;
Barbarians of man's simpler nature,
Unworldly servers of the world.
Yea, present all, and dear to me,
Though shades, or scouring China's sea.

Whither, whither, merchant-sailors,
Whitherward now in roaring gales?
Competing still, ye huntsman-whalers,
In leviathan's wake what boat prevails?
And man-of-war's men, whereaway?
If now no dinned drum beat to quarters
On the wilds of midnight waters—
Foemen looming through the spray;
Do yet your gangway lanterns, streaming,
Vainly strive to pierce below,
When, tilted from the slant plank gleaming,
A brother you see to darkness go?

But, gunmates lashed in shotted canvas,
If where long watch-below ye keep,
Never the shrill "All hands up hammocks!"
Breaks the spell that charms your sleep,
And summoning trumps might vainly call,
And booming guns implore—
A beat, a heart-beat musters all,
One heart-beat at heart-core.
It musters. But to clasp, retain;
To see you at the halyards main—
To hear your chorus once again!

THE WEST

A. E. Housman

Beyond the moor and the mountain crest
—Comrade, look not on the west—
The sun is down and drinks away
From air and land the lees of day.

The long cloud and the single pine
Sentinel the ending line,
And out beyond it, clear and wan,
Reach the gulfs of evening on.

The son of woman turns his brow
West from forty countries now,
And, as the edge of heaven he eyes,
Thinks eternal thoughts, and sighs.

Oh wide's the world, to rest or roam,
With change abroad and cheer at home,
Fights and furloughs, talk and tale,
Company and beef and ale.

But if I front the evening sky
Silent on the west look I,
And my comrade, stride for stride,
Paces silent at my side,

Comrade, look not on the west:
'Twill have the heart out of your breast;
'Twill take your thoughts and sink them far,
Leagues beyond the sunset bar.

Oh lad, I fear that yon's the sea
Where they fished for you and me,
And there, from whence we both were ta'en,
You and I shall drown again.

Send not on your soul before
To dive from that beguiling shore,
And let not yet the swimmer leave
His clothes upon the sands of eve.

Too fast to yonder strand forlorn
We journey, to the sunken bourn,
To flush the fading tinges eyed
By other lads at eventide.

Wide is the world, to rest or roam,
And early 'tis for turning home:
Plant your heel on earth and stand,
And let's forget our native land.

When you and I are split on air
Long we shall be strangers there;
Friends of flesh and bone are best;
Comrade, look not on the west.

SUNSET

Emily Dickinson

Where ships of purple gently toss
On seas of daffodil,
Fantastic sailors mingle,
And then — the wharf is still.

RIVER AND SEA

Ella Wheeler Wilcox

We stood by the river that swept
  In its glory and grandeur away;
But never a pulse o' me leapt,
  And you wondered at me that day.

We stood by the lake as it lay
  With its dimpled face turned to the light;
Was it strange I had nothing to say
  To so fair and enchanting a sight?

I look on your tresses of gold—
  You are fair and a thing to be loved—
Do you think I am heartless and cold
  That I look and am wholly unmoved?

One answer, dear friend, I will make
  To the questions your eyes ask of me:
"Talk not of the river or lake
  To those who have looked on the sea"

TWILIGHT

Heinrich Heine

On the wan shore of the sea
Lonely I sat with troubled thoughts.
The sun dropped lower, and cast
Glowing red streaks on the water.
And the white wide waves,
Crowding in with the tide,
Foamed and rustled, nearer and nearer,
With a strange rustling, a whispering, a hissing,
A laughter, a murmur, a sighing, a seething,
And amidst all these a mysterious lullaby.
I seemed to hear long-past traditions,
Lovely old-time fairy-tales,
Which as a boy I had heard,
From the neighbor's children,
When on summer evenings we had nestled
On the stone steps of the porch.

With little eager hearts,

And wistful cunning eyes,

Whilst the grown maidens

Sat opposite at their windows

Near their sweet-smelling flower pots,

With their rosy faces,

Smiling and beaming in the moonlight.

THE CAPTAIN'S DAUGHTER

James T. Fields

We were crowded in the cabin,
   Not a soul would dare to sleep,—
It was midnight on the waters,
   And a storm was on the deep.

'Tis a fearful thing in winter
   To be shattered by the blast,
And to hear the rattling trumpet
   Thunder, "Cut away the mast!"

So we shuddered there in silence,—
   For the stoutest held his breath,
While the hungry sea was roaring
   And the breakers talked with Death.

As thus we sat in darkness,
　　Each one busy with his prayers,
"We are lost!" the captain shouted
　　As he staggered down the stairs.

But his little daughter whispered,
　　As she took his icy hand,
"Isn't God upon the ocean,
　　Just the same as on the land?"

Then we kissed the little maiden.
　　And we spoke in better cheer,
And we anchored safe in harbour
　　When the morn was shining clear.

ANNABEL LEE

Edgar Allen Poe

It was many and many a year ago,
  In a kingdom by the sea,
That a maiden there lived whom you may know
  By the name of Annabel Lee;
And this maiden she lived with no other thought
  Than to love and be loved by me.

I was a child and she was a child,
  In this kingdom by the sea,
But we loved with a love that was more than love,
  I and my Annabel Lee;
With a love that the winged seraphs of heaven
  Coveted her and me.

And this was the reason that, long ago,
  In this kingdom by the sea,
A wind blew out of a cloud, chilling
  My beautiful Annabel Lee;

So that her highborn kinsmen came
  And bore her away from me,
To shut her up in a sepulchre
  In this kingdom by the sea.
The angels, not half so happy in heaven,
  Went envying her and me;
Yes! that was the reason (as all men know,
  In this kingdom by the sea)
That the wind came out of the cloud by night,
  Chilling and killing my Annabel Lee.
But our love it was stronger by far than the love
  Of those who were older than we,
  Of many far wiser than we;
And neither the angels in heaven above,
  Nor the demons down under the sea,
Can ever dissever my soul from the soul
  Of the beautiful Annabel Lee:
For the moon never beams, without bringing me dreams
  Of the beautiful Annabel Lee;
And the stars never rise, but I feel the bright eyes
  Of the beautiful Annabel Lee;
And so, all the night-tide, I lie down by the side
Of my darling—my darling—my life and my bride,
  In her sepulchre there by the sea,
  In her tomb by the sounding sea.

ENGLAND TO THE SEA

R. E. Vernède

Hearken, O Mother, hearken to thy daughter!
Fain would I tell thee what men tell to me,
Saying that henceforth no more on any water
Shall I be first or great or loved or free,

But that these others—so the tale is spoken—
Who have not known thee all these centuries
By fire and sword shall yet turn England broken
Back from thy breast and beaten from thy seas,

Me—whom thou barest where thy waves should guard me,
Me—whom thou suckled'st on thy milk of foam,
Me—whom thy kisses shaped what while they marred me,
To whom thy storms are sweet and ring of home.

"Behold," they cry, "she is grown soft and strengthless,

All her proud memories changed to fear and fret."
Say, thou, who hast watched through ages that are
   lengthless,
Whom have I feared, and when did I forget?

What sons of mine have shunned thy whorls and races?
Have I not reared for thee time and again
And bid go forth to share thy fierce embraces
Sea-ducks, sea-wolves, sea-rovers, and sea-men?

Names that thou knowest—great hearts that thou holdest,
Rocking them, rocking them in an endless wake—
Captains the world can match not with its boldest,
Hawke, Howard, Grenville, Frobisher, Drake?

Nelson—the greatest of them all—the master
Who swept across thee like a shooting star,
And, while the Earth stood veiled before disaster,
Caught Death and slew him—there—at Trafalgar?

Mother, they knew me then as thou didst know me;
Then I cried, Peace, and every flag was furled:
But I am old, it seems, and they would show me

That never more my peace shall bind the world.

Wherefore, O Sea, I, standing thus before thee,
Stretch forth my hands unto thy surge and say:
"When they come forth who seek this empire o'er thee,
And I go forth to meet them—on that day

"God grant to us the old Armada weather,
The winds that rip, the heavens that stoop and lour—
Not till the Sea and England sink together,
Shall they be masters! Let them boast that hour!"

THE FIGUREHEAD

Herman Melville

The *Charles-and-Emma* seaward sped,
(Named from the carven pair at prow,)
He so smart, and a curly head,
She tricked forth as a bride knows how:
Pretty stem for the port, I trow!

But iron-rust and alum-spray
And chafing gear, and sun and dew
Vexed this lad and lassie gay,
Tears in their eyes, salt tears nor few;
  And the hug relaxed with the failing glue.

But came in end a dismal night,
With creaking beams and ribs that groan,
A black lee-shore and waters white:
Dropped on the reef, the pair lie prone:
  O, the breakers dance, but the winds they
    moan!

SEA-HOARDINGS

Cale Young Rice

My heart is open again and sea flows in,
It shall fill with a summer of mists and winds and
    clouds and waves breaking,
Of gull-wings over the green tide, of the surf's
    drenching din,
Of sudden horizon-sails that come and vanish,
    phantom-thin,
Of arching sapphire skies, deep and unaching.
I shall lie on the rocks just over the weeds that drape
The clear sea-pools, where birth and death in sunny
    ooze are teeming.
Where the crab in quest of booty sidles about, a
    sullen shape,
Where the snail creeps and the mussel sleeps with
    wary valves agape,
Where life is too grotesque to be but seeming.
And the swallow shall weave my dreams with
    threads of flight,

A shuttle with silver breast across the warp of the
   waves gliding;
And an isle far out shall be a beam in the loom of
   my delight,
And the pattern of every dream shall be a rapture
   bathed in light—
Its evanescence a beauty most abiding.
And the sunsets shall give sadness all its due,
They shall stain the sands and trouble the tides with
   all the ache of sorrow.
They shall bleed and die with a beauty of meaning
   old yet ever new,
They shall burn with all the hunger for things that
   hearts have failed to do,
They shall whisper of a gold that none can borrow.
And the stars shall come and build a bridge of fire
For the moon to cross the boundless sea, with never
   a fear of sinking.
They shall teach me of the magic things of life never
   to tire,
And how to renew, when it is low, the lamp of my
   desire—
And how to hope, in the darkest deeps of thinking.

THE RIME OF THE ANCIENT MARINER

Samuel Taylor Coleridge

PART THE FIRST.

It is an ancient Mariner,
And he stoppeth one of three.
"By thy long grey beard and glittering eye,
Now wherefore stopp'st thou me?

"The Bridegroom's doors are opened wide,
And I am next of kin;
The guests are met, the feast is set:
May'st hear the merry din."

He holds him with his skinny hand,
"There was a ship," quoth he.
"Hold off! unhand me, grey-beard loon!"
Eftsoons his hand dropt he.

He holds him with his glittering eye—
The Wedding-Guest stood still,
And listens like a three years child:
The Mariner hath his will.

The Wedding-Guest sat on a stone:
He cannot chuse but hear;
And thus spake on that ancient man,
The bright-eyed Mariner.

The ship was cheered, the harbour cleared,
Merrily did we drop
Below the kirk, below the hill,
Below the light-house top.

The Sun came up upon the left,
Out of the sea came he!
And he shone bright, and on the right
Went down into the sea.

Higher and higher every day,
Till over the mast at noon—
The Wedding-Guest here beat his breast,

For he heard the loud bassoon.
The bride hath paced into the hall,
Red as a rose is she;
Nodding their heads before her goes
The merry minstrelsy.

The Wedding-Guest he beat his breast,
Yet he cannot chuse but hear;
And thus spake on that ancient man,
The bright-eyed Mariner.

And now the STORM-BLAST came, and he
Was tyrannous and strong:
He struck with his o'ertaking wings,
And chased south along.

With sloping masts and dipping prow,
As who pursued with yell and blow
Still treads the shadow of his foe
And forward bends his head,
The ship drove fast, loud roared the blast,
And southward aye we fled.

And now there came both mist and snow,

And it grew wondrous cold:
And ice, mast-high, came floating by,
As green as emerald.

And through the drifts the snowy clifts
Did send a dismal sheen:
Nor shapes of men nor beasts we ken—
The ice was all between.

The ice was here, the ice was there,
The ice was all around:
It cracked and growled, and roared and howled,
Like noises in a swound!

At length did cross an Albatross:
Thorough the fog it came;
As if it had been a Christian soul,
We hailed it in God's name.

It ate the food it ne'er had eat,
And round and round it flew.
The ice did split with a thunder-fit;
The helmsman steered us through!

And a good south wind sprung up behind;
The Albatross did follow,
And every day, for food or play,
Came to the mariners' hollo!

In mist or cloud, on mast or shroud,
It perched for vespers nine;
Whiles all the night, through fog-smoke white,
Glimmered the white Moon-shine.

"God save thee, ancient Mariner!
From the fiends, that plague thee thus!—
Why look'st thou so?"—With my cross-bow
I shot the ALBATROSS.

PART THE SECOND.

The Sun now rose upon the right:
Out of the sea came he,
Still hid in mist, and on the left
Went down into the sea.

And the good south wind still blew behind

But no sweet bird did follow,
Nor any day for food or play
Came to the mariners' hollo!
And I had done an hellish thing,
And it would work 'em woe:
For all averred, I had killed the bird
That made the breeze to blow.
Ah wretch! said they, the bird to slay
That made the breeze to blow!

Nor dim nor red, like God's own head,
The glorious Sun uprist:
Then all averred, I had killed the bird
That brought the fog and mist.
'Twas right, said they, such birds to slay,
That bring the fog and mist.

The fair breeze blew, the white foam flew,
The furrow followed free:
We were the first that ever burst
Into that silent sea.

Down dropt the breeze, the sails dropt down,
'Twas sad as sad could be;

And we did speak only to break
The silence of the sea!

All in a hot and copper sky,
The bloody Sun, at noon,
Right up above the mast did stand,
No bigger than the Moon.

Day after day, day after day,
We stuck, nor breath nor motion;
As idle as a painted ship
Upon a painted ocean.

Water, water, every where,
And all the boards did shrink;
Water, water, every where,
Nor any drop to drink.

The very deep did rot: O Christ!
That ever this should be!
Yea, slimy things did crawl with legs
Upon the slimy sea.

About, about, in reel and rout

The death-fires danced at night;
The water, like a witch's oils,
Burnt green, and blue and white.
And some in dreams assured were
Of the spirit that plagued us so:
Nine fathom deep he had followed us
From the land of mist and snow.

And every tongue, through utter drought,
Was withered at the root;
We could not speak, no more than if
We had been choked with soot.

Ah! well a-day! what evil looks
Had I from old and young!
Instead of the cross, the Albatross
About my neck was hung.

PART THE THIRD.

There passed a weary time. Each throat
Was parched, and glazed each eye.
A weary time! a weary time!
How glazed each weary eye,

When looking westward, I beheld
A something in the sky.

At first it seemed a little speck,
And then it seemed a mist:
It moved and moved, and took at last
A certain shape, I wist.

A speck, a mist, a shape, I wist!
And still it neared and neared:
As if it dodged a water-sprite,
It plunged and tacked and veered.

With throats unslaked, with black lips baked,
We could not laugh nor wail;
Through utter drought all dumb we stood!
I bit my arm, I sucked the blood,
And cried, A sail! a sail!

With throats unslaked, with black lips baked,
Agape they heard me call:
Gramercy! they for joy did grin,
And all at once their breath drew in,
As they were drinking all.

See! see! (I cried) she tacks no more!
Hither to work us weal;
Without a breeze, without a tide,
She steadies with upright keel!

The western wave was all a-flame
The day was well nigh done!
Almost upon the western wave
Rested the broad bright Sun;
When that strange shape drove suddenly
Betwixt us and the Sun.

And straight the Sun was flecked with bars,
(Heaven's Mother send us grace!)
As if through a dungeon-grate he peered,
With broad and burning face.

Alas! (thought I, and my heart beat loud)
How fast she nears and nears!
Are those her sails that glance in the Sun,
Like restless gossameres!

Are those her ribs through which the Sun
Did peer, as through a grate?
And is that Woman all her crew?

Is that a DEATH? and are there two?
Is DEATH that woman's mate?

Her lips were red, her looks were free,
Her locks were yellow as gold:
Her skin was as white as leprosy,
The Night-Mare LIFE-IN-DEATH was she,
Who thicks man's blood with cold.

The naked hulk alongside came,
And the twain were casting dice;
"The game is done! I've won! I've won!"
Quoth she, and whistles thrice.

The Sun's rim dips; the stars rush out:
At one stride comes the dark;
With far-heard whisper, o'er the sea.
Off shot the spectre-bark.

We listened and looked sideways up!
Fear at my heart, as at a cup,
My life-blood seemed to sip!

The stars were dim, and thick the night,
The steersman's face by his lamp gleamed white;

From the sails the dew did drip—
Till clombe above the eastern bar
The horned Moon, with one bright star
Within the nether tip.
One after one, by the star-dogged Moon
Too quick for groan or sigh,
Each turned his face with a ghastly pang,
And cursed me with his eye.

Four times fifty living men,
(And I heard nor sigh nor groan)
With heavy thump, a lifeless lump,
They dropped down one by one.

The souls did from their bodies fly,—
They fled to bliss or woe!
And every soul, it passed me by,
Like the whizz of my CROSS-BOW!

PART THE FOURTH.

"I fear thee, ancient Mariner!
I fear thy skinny hand!
And thou art long, and lank, and brown,

As is the ribbed sea-sand.

"I fear thee and thy glittering eye,
And thy skinny hand, so brown."—
Fear not, fear not, thou Wedding-Guest!
This body dropt not down.
Alone, alone, all, all alone,
Alone on a wide wide sea!
And never a saint took pity on
My soul in agony.

The many men, so beautiful!
And they all dead did lie:
And a thousand thousand slimy things
Lived on; and so did I.

I looked upon the rotting sea,
And drew my eyes away;
I looked upon the rotting deck,
And there the dead men lay.

I looked to Heaven, and tried to pray:
But or ever a prayer had gusht,
A wicked whisper came, and made
my heart as dry as dust.

I closed my lids, and kept them close,
And the balls like pulses beat;
For the sky and the sea, and the sea and the sky
Lay like a load on my weary eye,
And the dead were at my feet.
The cold sweat melted from their limbs,
Nor rot nor reek did they:
The look with which they looked on me
Had never passed away.

An orphan's curse would drag to Hell
A spirit from on high;
But oh! more horrible than that
Is a curse in a dead man's eye!
Seven days, seven nights, I saw that curse,
And yet I could not die.

The moving Moon went up the sky,
And no where did abide:
Softly she was going up,
And a star or two beside.

Her beams bemocked the sultry main,
Like April hoar-frost spread;

But where the ship's huge shadow lay,
The charmed water burnt alway
A still and awful red.

Beyond the shadow of the ship,
I watched the water-snakes:
They moved in tracks of shining white,
And when they reared, the elfish light
Fell off in hoary flakes.

Within the shadow of the ship
I watched their rich attire:
Blue, glossy green, and velvet black,
They coiled and swam; and every track
Was a flash of golden fire.

O happy living things! no tongue
Their beauty might declare:
A spring of love gushed from my heart,
And I blessed them unaware:
Sure my kind saint took pity on me,
And I blessed them unaware.

The self same moment I could pray;
And from my neck so free

The Albatross fell off, and sank
Like lead into the sea.

PART THE FIFTH.

Oh sleep! it is a gentle thing,
Beloved from pole to pole!
To Mary Queen the praise be given!
She sent the gentle sleep from Heaven,
That slid into my soul.

The silly buckets on the deck,
That had so long remained,
I dreamt that they were filled with dew;
And when I awoke, it rained.

My lips were wet, my throat was cold,
My garments all were dank;
Sure I had drunken in my dreams,
And still my body drank.

I moved, and could not feel my limbs:
I was so light—almost
I thought that I had died in sleep,
And was a blessed ghost.

And soon I heard a roaring wind:
It did not come anear;
But with its sound it shook the sails,
That were so thin and sere.
The upper air burst into life!
And a hundred fire-flags sheen,
To and fro they were hurried about!
And to and fro, and in and out,
The wan stars danced between.

And the coming wind did roar more loud,
And the sails did sigh like sedge;
And the rain poured down from one black cloud;
The Moon was at its edge.

The thick black cloud was cleft, and still
The Moon was at its side:
Like waters shot from some high crag,
The lightning fell with never a jag,
A river steep and wide.
The loud wind never reached the ship,
Yet now the ship moved on!
Beneath the lightning and the Moon
The dead men gave a groan.

They groaned, they stirred, they all uprose,
Nor spake, nor moved their eyes;
It had been strange, even in a dream,
To have seen those dead men rise.

The helmsman steered, the ship moved on;
Yet never a breeze up blew;
The mariners all 'gan work the ropes,
Where they were wont to do:
They raised their limbs like lifeless tools—
We were a ghastly crew.

The body of my brother's son,
Stood by me, knee to knee:
The body and I pulled at one rope,
But he said nought to me.

"I fear thee, ancient Mariner!"
Be calm, thou Wedding-Guest!
'Twas not those souls that fled in pain,
Which to their corses came again,
But a troop of spirits blest:

For when it dawned—they dropped their arms,
And clustered round the mast;

Sweet sounds rose slowly through their mouths,
And from their bodies passed.

Around, around, flew each sweet sound,
Then darted to the Sun;
Slowly the sounds came back again,
Now mixed, now one by one.

Sometimes a-dropping from the sky
I heard the sky-lark sing;
Sometimes all little birds that are,
How they seemed to fill the sea and air
With their sweet jargoning!

And now 'twas like all instruments,
Now like a lonely flute;
And now it is an angel's song,
That makes the Heavens be mute.

It ceased; yet still the sails made on
A pleasant noise till noon,
A noise like of a hidden brook
In the leafy month of June,

That to the sleeping woods all night
Singeth a quiet tune.

Till noon we quietly sailed on,
Yet never a breeze did breathe:
Slowly and smoothly went the ship,
Moved onward from beneath.

Under the keel nine fathom deep,
From the land of mist and snow,
The spirit slid: and it was he
That made the ship to go.
The sails at noon left off their tune,
And the ship stood still also.

The Sun, right up above the mast,
Had fixed her to the ocean:
But in a minute she 'gan stir,
With a short uneasy motion—
Backwards and forwards half her length
With a short uneasy motion.

Then like a pawing horse let go,
She made a sudden bound:

It flung the blood into my head,
And I fell down in a swound.
How long in that same fit I lay,
I have not to declare;
But ere my living life returned,
I heard and in my soul discerned
Two VOICES in the air.

"Is it he?" quoth one, "Is this the man?
By him who died on cross,
With his cruel bow he laid full low,
The harmless Albatross.

"The spirit who bideth by himself
In the land of mist and snow,
He loved the bird that loved the man
Who shot him with his bow."

The other was a softer voice,
As soft as honey-dew:
Quoth he, "The man hath penance done,
And penance more will do."

PART THE SIXTH.

FIRST VOICE.
But tell me, tell me! speak again,
Thy soft response renewing—
What makes that ship drive on so fast?
What is the OCEAN doing?
SECOND VOICE.

Still as a slave before his lord,
The OCEAN hath no blast;
His great bright eye most silently
Up to the Moon is cast—

If he may know which way to go;
For she guides him smooth or grim
See, brother, see! how graciously
She looketh down on him.
FIRST VOICE.

But why drives on that ship so fast,
Without or wave or wind?
SECOND VOICE.

The air is cut away before,
And closes from behind.
Fly, brother, fly! more high, more high
Or we shall be belated:
For slow and slow that ship will go,
When the Mariner's trance is abated.

I woke, and we were sailing on
As in a gentle weather:
'Twas night, calm night, the Moon was high;
The dead men stood together.

All stood together on the deck,
For a charnel-dungeon fitter:
All fixed on me their stony eyes,
That in the Moon did glitter.

The pang, the curse, with which they died,
Had never passed away:
I could not draw my eyes from theirs,
Nor turn them up to pray.

And now this spell was snapt: once more
I viewed the ocean green.

And looked far forth, yet little saw
Of what had else been seen—
Like one that on a lonesome road
Doth walk in fear and dread,
And having once turned round walks on,
And turns no more his head;
Because he knows, a frightful fiend
Doth close behind him tread.

But soon there breathed a wind on me,
Nor sound nor motion made:
Its path was not upon the sea,
In ripple or in shade.

It raised my hair, it fanned my cheek
Like a meadow-gale of spring—
It mingled strangely with my fears,
Yet it felt like a welcoming.

Swiftly, swiftly flew the ship,
Yet she sailed softly too:
Sweetly, sweetly blew the breeze—
On me alone it blew.

Oh! dream of joy! is this indeed
The light-house top I see?
Is this the hill? is this the kirk?
Is this mine own countree!

We drifted o'er the harbour-bar,
And I with sobs did pray—
O let me be awake, my God!
Or let me sleep alway.

The harbour-bay was clear as glass,
So smoothly it was strewn!
And on the bay the moonlight lay,
And the shadow of the moon.

The rock shone bright, the kirk no less,
That stands above the rock:
The moonlight steeped in silentness
The steady weathercock.

And the bay was white with silent light,
Till rising from the same,
Full many shapes, that shadows were,
In crimson colours came.

A little distance from the prow
Those crimson shadows were:
I turned my eyes upon the deck—
Oh, Christ! what saw I there!

Each corse lay flat, lifeless and flat,
And, by the holy rood!
A man all light, a seraph-man,
On every corse there stood.

This seraph band, each waved his hand:
It was a heavenly sight!
They stood as signals to the land,
Each one a lovely light:

This seraph-band, each waved his hand,
No voice did they impart—
No voice; but oh! the silence sank
Like music on my heart.

But soon I heard the dash of oars;
I heard the Pilot's cheer;
My head was turned perforce away,
And I saw a boat appear.

The Pilot, and the Pilot's boy,
I heard them coming fast:
Dear Lord in Heaven! it was a joy
The dead men could not blast.

I saw a third—I heard his voice:
It is the Hermit good!
He singeth loud his godly hymns
That he makes in the wood.
He'll shrieve my soul, he'll wash away
The Albatross's blood.

PART THE SEVENTH.

This Hermit good lives in that wood
Which slopes down to the sea.
How loudly his sweet voice he rears!
He loves to talk with marineres
That come from a far countree.

He kneels at morn and noon and eve—
He hath a cushion plump:
It is the moss that wholly hides
The rotted old oak-stump.

The skiff-boat neared: I heard them talk,
"Why this is strange, I trow!
Where are those lights so many and fair,
That signal made but now?"

"Strange, by my faith!" the Hermit said—
"And they answered not our cheer!
The planks looked warped! and see those sails,
How thin they are and sere!
I never saw aught like to them,
Unless perchance it were

"Brown skeletons of leaves that lag
My forest-brook along;
When the ivy-tod is heavy with snow,
And the owlet whoops to the wolf below,
That eats the she-wolf's young."

"Dear Lord! it hath a fiendish look—
(The Pilot made reply)
I am a-feared"—"Push on, push on!"
Said the Hermit cheerily.

The boat came closer to the ship,

But I nor spake nor stirred;
The boat came close beneath the ship,
And straight a sound was heard.

Under the water it rumbled on,
Still louder and more dread:
It reached the ship, it split the bay;
The ship went down like lead.

Stunned by that loud and dreadful sound,
Which sky and ocean smote,
Like one that hath been seven days drowned
My body lay afloat;
But swift as dreams, myself I found
Within the Pilot's boat.

Upon the whirl, where sank the ship,
The boat spun round and round;
And all was still, save that the hill
Was telling of the sound.

I moved my lips—the Pilot shrieked
And fell down in a fit;

The holy Hermit raised his eyes,
And prayed where he did sit.

I took the oars: the Pilot's boy,
Who now doth crazy go,
Laughed loud and long, and all the while
His eyes went to and fro.
"Ha! ha!" quoth he, "full plain I see,
The Devil knows how to row."

And now, all in my own countree,
I stood on the firm land!
The Hermit stepped forth from the boat,
And scarcely he could stand.

"O shrieve me, shrieve me, holy man!"
The Hermit crossed his brow.
"Say quick," quoth he, "I bid thee say—
What manner of man art thou?"

Forthwith this frame of mine was wrenched
With a woeful agony,
Which forced me to begin my tale;

And then it left me free.
Since then, at an uncertain hour,
That agony returns;
And till my ghastly tale is told,
This heart within me burns.

I pass, like night, from land to land;
I have strange power of speech;
That moment that his face I see,
I know the man that must hear me:
To him my tale I teach.

What loud uproar bursts from that door!
The wedding-guests are there:
But in the garden-bower the bride
And bride-maids singing are:
And hark the little vesper bell,
Which biddeth me to prayer!

O Wedding-Guest! this soul hath been
Alone on a wide wide sea:
So lonely 'twas, that God himself
Scarce seemed there to be.

O sweeter than the marriage-feast,
'Tis sweeter far to me,
To walk together to the kirk
With a goodly company!—

To walk together to the kirk,
And all together pray,
While each to his great Father bends,
Old men, and babes, and loving friends,
And youths and maidens gay!

Farewell, farewell! but this I tell
To thee, thou Wedding-Guest!
He prayeth well, who loveth well
Both man and bird and beast.

He prayeth best, who loveth best
All things both great and small;
For the dear God who loveth us
He made and loveth all.

The Mariner, whose eye is bright,
Whose beard with age is hoar,
Is gone: and now the Wedding-Guest
Turned from the bridegroom's door.

He went like one that hath been stunned,

And is of sense forlorn:

A sadder and a wiser man,

He rose the morrow morn.

TO THE MASTER OF THE METEOR

Herman Melville

Lonesome on earth's loneliest deep,
Sailor! who dost thy vigil keep—
Off the Cape of Storms dost musing sweep
Over monstrous waves that curl and comb;
Of thee we think when here from brink
We blow the mead in bubbling foam.

Of thee we think, in a ring we link;
To the shearer of ocean's fleece we drink,
And the *Meteor* rolling home.

UNRETURNING

Emily Dickinson

'T was such a little, little boat
That toddled down the bay!
'T was such a gallant, gallant sea
That beckoned it away!

'T was such a greedy, greedy wave
That licked it from the coast;
Nor ever guessed the stately sails
My little craft was lost!

CROSSING THE BAR

Alfred, Lord Tennyson

Sunset and evening star,
    And one clear call for me!
And may there be no moaning of the bar,
    When I put out to sea,

But such a tide as moving seems asleep,
    Too full for sound and foam,
When that which drew from out the boundless deep
    Turns again home.

Twilight and evening bell,
    And after that the dark!
And may there be no sadness of farewell,
    When I embark;

For tho' from out our bourne of Time and Place
    The flood may bear me far,
I hope to see my Pilot face to face
    When I have cross'd the bar.

SALUTATION TO
THE SEA

Heinrich Heine

Thalatta! Thalatta!
All hail to thee, thou Eternal sea!
All hail to thee ten thousand times
From my jubilant heart,
As once thou wast hailed
By ten thousand Grecian hearts,
Misfortune-combating, homeward-yearning,
World-renowned Grecian hearts.
The waters heaved,
They heaved and roared.
The sun poured streaming downward
Its flickering rosy lights.
The startled flocks of sea-mews
Fluttered away with shrill screams;
The coursers stamped, the shields rattled,

And far out, resounded like a triumphal pæan,

Thalatta! Thalatta!

All hail to thee, thou Eternal Sea!

Like the language of home, thy water whispers to me.

Like the dreams of my childhood I see it glimmer.

Over thy billowy realm of waves.

And it repeats to me anew olden memories,

Of all the belovèd glorious sports,

Of all the twinkling Christmas gifts,

Of all the ruddy coral-trees,

Tiny golden fishes, pearls and bright-hued mussels,

Which thou dost secretly preserve

Below there in thy limpid house of crystal.

Oh, how I have pined in barren exile!

Like a withered flower

In the tin box of a botanist,

My heart lay in my breast.

I feel as if all winter I had sat,

A sick man, in a dark, sick room,

Which now I suddenly leave.

And dazzlingly shines down upon me

The emerald spring, the sunshine-awakened spring,

And the white-blossomed trees are rustling;

And the young flowers look at me,

With their many-colored, fragrant eyes.

And there is an aroma, and a murmuring, and a
  breathing and a laughter,

And in the blue sky the little birds are singing,

Thalatta! Thalatta!

Thou valiant, retreating heart,

How oft, how bitter oft

Did the fair barbarians of the North press thee hard!

From their large victorious eyes

They darted burning shafts.

With crooked, polished words,

They threatened to cleave my breast.

With sharp-pointed missives they shattered

My poor, stunned brain.

In vain I held up against them my shield,

The arrows whizzed, the strokes cracked,

And from the fair barbarians of the North

I was pressed even unto the sea.

And now with deep, free breath, I hail the sea,

The dear, redeeming sea—

Thalatta! Thalatta!

THE SEA

Emily Dickinson

An everywhere of silver,
With ropes of sand
To keep it from effacing
The track called land.

THE FAIRIES OF GOD

Cale Young Rice

Last night I slipt from the banks of dream
And swam in the currents of God,
On a tide where His fairies were at play,
Catching salt tears in their little white hands,
For human hearts;
And dancing, dancing, in gala bands,
On the currents of God;
And singing, singing:—

There is no wind blows here or spray—
Wind upon us!
Only the waters ripple away
Under our feet as we gather tears.
God has made mortals for the years,
Us for alway!
God has made mortals full of fears,
Fears for the night and fears for the day.

If they would free them of grief that sears,
If they would keep what love endears,
If they would lay no more lilies on biers—
Let them say!
For we are swift to enchant and tire
Time's will!
Our feet are wiser than all desire,
Our song is better than faith or fame;
To whom it is given no ill e'er came,
Who has it not grows chill!
Who has it not grows laggard and lame,
Nor knows that the world is a Minstrel's lyre,
Smitten and never still!...

Last night on the currents of God.

ABOUT BUSHEL & PECK BOOKS

Bushel & Peck Books is a children's publishing house with a special mission. Through our Book-for-Book Promise™, we donate one book to kids in need for every book we sell. Our beautiful books are given to kids through schools, libraries, local neighborhoods, shelters, nonprofits, and also to many selfless organizations that are working hard to make a difference. So thank you for purchasing this book! Because of you, another book will make its way into the hands of a child who needs it most.

NOMINATE A SCHOOL OR ORGANIZATION TO RECEIVE FREE BOOKS

Do you know a school, library, or organization that could use some free books for their kids? We'd love to help! Please fill out the nomination form on our website (see below), and we'll do everything we can to make something happen.

www.bushelandpeckbooks.com/pages/
nominate-a-school-or-organization

If you liked this book, please leave a review online at your favorite retailer. Honest reviews spread the word about Bushel & Peck—and help us make better books, too!